Thomas Hardy's Dors

Thomas Hardy's Dorset

> " *To recline on a stump of thorn in the central valley of Egdon, between afternoon and night, as now, where the eye could reach nothing of the world outside the summits and shoulders of heathland which filled the whole circumference of its glance, and to know that everything around and underneath had been from prehistoric times as unaltered as the stars overhead, gave ballast to the mind adrift on change...* "

Return of the Native

AMBASSADOR |

SALMON

Published by J Salmon Limited
100 London Road, Sevenoaks, Kent TN13 1BB

First edition 1999
Second edition 2003

Designed by the Salmon Studio

Printed in England by
J Salmon Limited, Tubs Hill Works, Sevenoaks, Kent

Front cover: Dorset coast at Durdle Door
Back cover: Thomas Hardy's Birthplace
Half title page: Hardy's memorial, Dorchester
Title page: Abbey Street, Cerne Abbas

Weymouth Harbour

Introduction

The Wessex of Thomas Hardy's novels ranges, in its widest sense, from, in the west the Cornish village of Boscastle, the "Castle Boterel" of A Pair of Blue Eyes, to Windsor, called by him "Castle Royal", in the east, and is bounded in the north by the Thames Valley. However, his excursions into the neighbourhood of Oxford ("Christminster") are comparatively few, nor does he often cross the Devon, Somerset and Wiltshire borders to places which are easily identifiable. The true heart of Hardy's Wessex lies exclusively within the boundaries of Dorset, principally around the county town of Dorchester, which was renamed "Casterbridge."

Hereabouts hidden valleys which shelter ancient farmsteads and picturesque villages rise up into windswept sharply cut hills, devoid of vegetation save for gorse and heather. On these heights nature wears an austere expression and the face of the landscape has changed little since the days of primitive man, who lived there long before the Saxons drove their longships onto Chesil Bank or Alfred battled the Danes in Swanage Bay. Hardy's fine description of Egdon Heath in The Return of the Native dwells upon these unchanging and unchangeable aspects. He writes of the "swarthy and abrupt slopes", approached by "a wildhill that had no name, beside a barren down that never looked like summer".

It was Hardy's genius which brought the essential soul of Dorset to life and made this most beautiful corner of rural England something universal; well-known and accessible to all. In the towns and villages of Dorset Hardy found fitting and effective backgrounds for the action of his tragic stories, and in them opportunity for the exercise of his unrivalled powers of description. From this landscape he drew many of his most interesting characters made more convincing because they spring naturally from their native environment and inhabit places which are readily recognisable even today.

Desribed below are the principal towns and villages which feature in Hardy's works. There are many other hamlets, farmhouses and manor houses which appear briefly and are too numerous to mention.

Affpuddle	*East Egdon*
Beaminster	*Emminster*
Bere Heath	*Egdon Heath*
Bere Regis	*Kingsbere*
Blandford Forum	*Shottsford Forum*
Bournemouth	*Sandbourne*
Bridport	*Port Bredy*
Cerne Abbas	*Abbot's Cernal*
Corfe Castle	*Corvesgate Castle*
Cranborne	*Chaseborough*
Dorchester	*Casterbridge*
Evershot	*Evershed*
Gillingham	*Leddenton*
Lulworth Cove	*Lulstead Cove*
Marlott	*Marnhull*
Milton Abbas	*Middleton Abbey*
Okeford Fitzpaine	*Oakbury Fitzpiers*
Poole	*Havenpool*
Portland	*Isle of Slingers*
Puddletown	*Weatherbury*
Shaftesbury	*Shaston*
Sherborne	*Sherton Abbas*
Stinsford	*Lower Mellstock*
Sutton Poyntz	*Overcombe*
Sturminster Newton	*Stourcastle*
Swanage	*Knollsea*
Tindeton	*Stickleford*
Tolpuddle	*Tolchurch*
Wareham	*Anglebury*
Weymouth	*Budmouth Regis*
Wimborne	*Warborne*
Wool	*Wellbridge*

The Gardens, Forde Abbey ▷

The bustling county town of **Dorchester** features in Thomas Hardy's novels as "Casterbridge" and it still has a busy market which attracts people from a wide area, as it did in Hardy's time. The impressive Tudor building in the High Street is reputed to have been where the infamous Judge Jeffreys lodged when he held the "Bloody Assizes" in 1685 following the defeat of Monmouth's rebellion. Two miles south-west of Dorchester the massive Iron Age hill fort of **Maiden Castle** dominates the landscape for miles around. The site was first fortified about 300 BC and by the time the Romans invaded Britain in the first century AD, some 5000 people could be contained within the earthen ramparts. The fort was abandoned after a successful Roman attack in 43 AD but centuries later it was used as a pagan temple.

" *Its squareness was, indeed, the characteristic which most struck the eye in this antiquated borough, the borough of Casterbridge... . It was compact as a box of dominoes. It had no suburbs – in the ordinary sense. Country and town met at a mathematical line. To birds of the more soaring kind Casterbridge must have appeared on this fine evening as a mosaic-work of subdued reds, browns, greys, and crystals, held together by a rectangular frame of deep green. To the level eye of humanity it stood as an indistinct mass behind a dense stockade of limes and chestnuts, set in the midst of miles of rotund down and concave field. The mass became gradually dissected by the vision into towers, gables, chimneys, and casements, the highest glazings shining bleared and boodshot with the coppery fire they caught from the belt of sunlit cloud in the west.* "

The Mayor of Casterbridge

◁ Maiden Castle
Judge Jeffrey's Lodgings, Dorchester ▷

In this pretty thatched cottage, tucked away in the hamlet of **Higher Bockhampton**, Thomas Hardy was born in 1840. It was while he was still living here that he wrote *Under the Greenwood Tree* and *Far from the Madding Crowd*. The cottage, which lies on the edge of the wild and primitive moorland which he called Egdon Heath, was built by the novelist's great-grandfather. At the nearby village of **Stinsford**, the Mellstock of Hardy's novels, stands the 13th century Church of St. Michael. Although Thomas Hardy was buried in Westminster Abbey, his heart was placed in a grave in Stinsford churchyard.

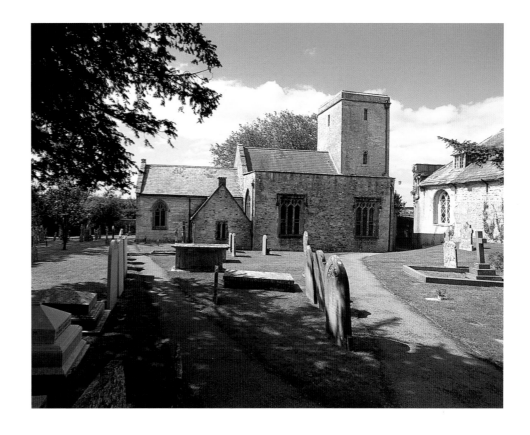

The three left the door and paced down Mellstock-lane and across the ewe-lease, bearing under their arms the instruments in faded green-baize bags, and old brown music-books in their hands.... At the foot of an incline the church became visible through the north gate, or 'church hatch', as it was called here. Seven agile figures in a clump were observable beyond, which proved to be the choristers waiting; sitting on an altar-tomb to pass the time, and letting their heels dangle against it. The musicians now being in sight the youthful party scampered off and rattled up the old wooden stairs of the gallery like a regiment of cavalry; the other boys of the parish waiting outside and observing birds, cats, and other creatures till the vicar entered, when they suddenly subsided into sober church-goers, and passed down the aisle with echoing heels.

Under the Greenwood Tree

◁ Hardy's Birthplace
Stinsford Church ▷

Regarded as pioneers of the trades union movement, the Tolpuddle Martyrs were sentanced to transportation in 1834 for uniting to resist a reduction in their wages as farm-workers. The village of **Tolpuddle** contains a number of memorials to the men including a small museum and six cottages known as "The Martyrs" which were built by the Trades Union Congress to mark the centenary of this historic event. One of the martyrs lies buried in the graveyard where there is also a headstone to the martyrs, designed by the sculptor and engraver Eric Gill. Situated some five miles north-east of Dorchester, **Athelhampton** is one of the finest of Dorset's many stately homes and manor houses. It dates from the 15th century and has an outstanding medieval hall with linenfold panelling, a minstrels' gallery and a heraldic glass window. The house is surrounded by a series of gardens which include a dovecot, fishponds and the Topiary Garden with its pyramid shaped yews.

They gave up their lodgings at Budmouth, and went to Tolchurch as soon as the work commenced. Here they were domiciled in one half of an old farm-house, standing not far from the ivy-covered church tower (which was all that was to remain of the original structure). The long steep roof of this picturesque dwelling sloped nearly down to the ground, the old tiles that covered it being overgrown with rich olive-hued moss. New red tiles in twos and threes had been used for patching the holes wrought by decay, lighting up the whole harmonious surface with dots of brilliant scarlet.

Desperate Remedies

◁ James Hammett's grave, Tolpuddle
The Topiary Garden, Athelhampton ▷

The heathland of central Dorset features in the novels of Thomas Hardy and is studded with quiet little villages which have changed little since he wrote about them. **Moreton**, with its picturesque thatched cottages, is also associated with T. E. Lawrence, better known as 'Lawrence of Arabia', who lived nearby. He was killed in a motor-cycle accident in 1935 and is buried in the churchyard of the beautiful little church of St. Nicholas at Moreton. Lawrence bought **Clouds Hill**, which lies between Wareham and Dorchester, as a retreat in 1925. The game-keeper's cottage which he called "an earthly paradise" is now owned by the National Trust.

◁ Clouds Hill
Moreton Village ▷

They entered Anglebury Station in the dead, still time of early morning, the clock over the booking-office pointing to twenty-five minutes to three. ... It was a raw, damp, uncomfortable morning, though, as yet, little rain was falling. Manston drank a mouthful from his flask and walked at once away from the station, pursuing his way through the gloom till he stood at the entrance to the town adjoining, at a distance from the last house in the street of about two hundred yards. The station road was also the turnpike-road into the country, the first part of its course being across a heath. ...The drizzling rain increased, and drops from the trees at the wayside fell noisily upon the hard road beneath them, which reflected from its glassy surface the faint halo of light hanging over the lamps of the adjacent town.

Desperate Remedies

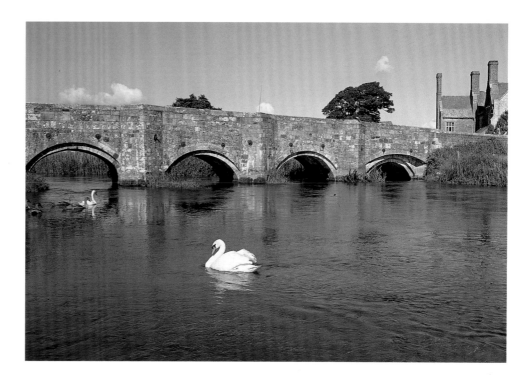

The delightful old town of **Wareham**, Hardy's "Anglebury", is situated at the head of the River Frome and is a popular centre for fishermen and small boat enthusiasts. An important settlement in Saxon times, Wareham suffered at the hands of the Danes and again during the Civil War. St. Martin's Church dates from Saxon times and contains an effigy of Lawrence of Arabia who lived nearby. The attractive village of **Wool** also stands on the River Frome, surrounded by water meadows and heathland. The 17th century bridge which spans the river is one of the finest in the county. It bears a rare transportation tablet threatening deportation as the penalty for misdemeanours such as driving an overloaded cart across the bridge. Hardy named the village "Wellbridge" and in the manor house Angel Clare and Tess of the d'Urbervilles spend their brief honeymoon.

◁ St. Martin's Church, Wareham
The Bridge and River Frome, Wool ▷

Once it was no more than a little fishing village but **Swanage**, Hardy's "Knollsea", has now grown into a popular seaside resort offering a safe bathing beach and good anchorage for yachts. Sheltered to the north by the high chalk cliffs of Ballard Down, the town lies at the southern end of a semi-circular sandy bay which was the scene of a famous battle in 877AD when King Alfred defeated a Danish fleet. There are many reminders of the old part of the town, particularly in the area around the mill pond which is surrounded by attractive stone-built cottages and overlooked by the church with its sturdy 13th century tower. The ancient village of **Corfe Castle**, "Corvesgate Castle", in The Hand of Ethelberta, built of local grey Purbeck stone, is dominated by the majestic ruins of its castle. Originally a Norman structure, it was built to guard a gap in the Purbeck Hills. The present castle dates from the 15th century and remained intact until it fell to Cromwell's troops during the Civil War.

◁ Swanage from the Downs
Corfe Castle ▷

To the east of Corfe Castle a road leads out to Studland, a pretty village set in a secluded bay close to the sea, downs and woods. At the southern end of the bay is the spit of land called The Foreland off which stand the isolated chalk stacks known as **Old Harry Rocks**. These prominent landmarks have been eroded from the cliffs by the action of the wind and waves. Between Durlston Head and St. Aldhelm's Head the Dorset Coast Path offers magnificent views along this rugged stretch of the cliffs where many a ship has foundered on the rocks. **Seacombe Ledges** can be reached by a footpath from the tranquil village of Worth Matravers.

" *...the windy, sousing, thwacking, basting, scourging Jack Ketch of a corner called Old Harry Point, which lay about midway along the track, and stood with its detached posts and stumps of white rock like a skeleton's lower jaw grinning at British Navigation!* "

Hand of Ethelberta

◁ Old Harry Rocks
Seacombe Ledges ▷

He descended and came to a small basin of sea enclosed by the cliffs. Troy's nature freshened within him; he thought he would rest and bathe here before going further. He undressed and plunged in. Inside the cove the water was uninteresting to a swimmer, being smooth as a pond, and to get a little of the ocean swell Troy presently swam between the two projecting spurs of rock which formed the pillars of Hercules to this miniature Mediterranean.

Far from the Madding Crowd

The chalk downs of Dorset meet the sea at **Lulworth**, Hardy's "Lulstead", in an impressive stretch of coastline. The high white cliffs are indented with sandy coves and clifftop paths provide superb views in every direction. Lulworth Cove, one of England's most photographed spots, is nearly circular in shape. West of the famous cove is the spectacular natural arch of rock known as **Durdle Door**. It takes its name from the Anglo-Saxon word "thirl", meaning "to pierce" and was created by the action of the sea over a period of time wearing away soft rock to leave an arch of harder Portland stone. Standing 40 feet high, it is reached by a steep path which runs down to a little cove of crystal clear water.

◁ The coast near Lulworth
Durdle Door from Swyre Head ▷

Immediately before her was the large, smooth mill-pond, over-full, and intruding into the hedge and into the road. The water, with its flowing leaves and spots of froth, was stealing away, like Time, under the dark arch, to tumble over the great slimy wheel within. The upland by its height completely sheltered the mill and village from north winds, making summers of springs, reducing winters to autumn temperatures, and permitting myrtles to flourish in the open air.

The Trumpet Major

Lying snugly between the downs and the sea **Osmington** offers fine views across Weymouth Bay. With its picturesque thatched cottages it is typical of the peaceful little villages of south Dorset. Osmington is famous for the huge chalk figure, an equestrian representation of George III, which was cut into the nearby hillside in 1808. Nestling among hills a short distance inland from Weymouth Bay, the charming little village of **Sutton Poyntz** plays a prominent part in Thomas Hardy's novel *The Trumpet Major,* in which it is known as Overcombe. Around the pond stand a number of fine old cottages, several of them thatched, which are typical of the architecture of the area.

◁ Sutton Poyntz
White Horse, Osmington ▷

The boats, the sands, the esplanade,
The laughing crowd;
Light-hearted, loud
Greetings from some not ill-endowed;

The evening sunlit cliffs, the talk,
Hailings and halts,
The keen sea-salts,
The band, the Morgenblätter Waltz.

Poem written at Weymouth

George III first popularised sea-bathing at **Weymouth**, which Hardy renamed "Budmouth Regis", in 1789 and it is now one of the principal resorts on the south coast with a long sweeping sandy beach and fine promenade where an ornate clock tower was erected in 1887 to mark Queen Victoria's golden jubilee. Fishing boats and pleasure craft still mingle with commercial vessels in the busy harbour which was a target for considerable bombing during the Second World War. The glorious curve of Weymouth Bay is one of the finest on the south coast. It is sheltered by the Isle of Portland, "The Isle of Slingers", a limestone peninsula which stretches out into the English Channel connected to the mainland only by a narrow neck of land. The 136 feet high lighthouse which was built between 1903 and 1906 to replace two earlier structures, stands on **Portland Bill**, the island's southernmost tip, warning shipping away from the dangerous channels.

◁ Weymouth Harbour, evening
Sunset at Portland Bill ▷

" They sheared in the great barn ... which on ground-plan resembled a church without transepts... The vast porches at the sides, lofty enough to admit a waggon laden to its highest with corn in the sheaf, were spanned by heavy-pointed arches of stone, broadly and boldly cut... Along each side wall was a range of striding buttresses throwing deep shadows on the spaces between them. "

Far from the Madding Crowd

Situated in a valley of outstanding natural beauty, **Abbotsbury** is an ancient village of thatched, stone-built houses. It is famous for its swannery, situated on the long strip of water behind Chesil Beach. Swans were first kept here 600 years ago to provide fresh food for the abbey and this is now the only managed nesting colony of mute swans in Britain. The Benedictine monks who established the famous swannery also built the magnificent tithe barn which was used to store all the grain produced throughout the neighbouring area. Dating from the 15th century, it is one of the largest and finest tithe barns in the country with an overall length of 272 feet. Hardy used it as the setting for the famous sheep-shearing scene in *Far from the Madding Crowd.*

◁ Chesil Beach
The Tithe Barn, Abbotsbury ▷

> *A person who differed from the local wayfarers was climbing the steep road which leads through the sea-skirted townlet definable as the Street of Wells, and forms a pass into that Gibraltar of Wessex, the singular peninsula once an island, and still called such, that stretches out like the head of a bird into the English Channel. It is connected with the mainland by a long thin neck of pebbles 'cast up by rages of the sea,' and unparalleled in its kind in Europe.*

The Well-beloved

Stretching some ten miles from Abbotsbury to the Isle of Portland, **Chesil Bank** is one of Britain's most remarkable natural features. Taking its name from the Saxon word for 'shingle', it is part of a pebble ridge which continues as far as Bridport and one of its intriguing features is that the pebbles are automatically graduated in size, becoming larger as the bank sweeps eastwards. More than forty feet high in places, it forms a natural break-water which protects Weymouth from storms blowing across West Bay. It has been formed over many thousands of years and is one of the longest pebble ridges in Europe. From Burton Cliff, at the western extremity of the ridge, there are fine views which extend as far as Portland Bill and take in the hamlet of West Bexington which is a favourite spot for fishing enthusiasts.

◁ Chesil Beach from Burton Cliff
Chesil Beach at West Bexington ▷

The rolling chalk hills which stretch across west Dorset look down upon fertile valleys watered by numerous rivers and streams. Midway between Dorchester and Bridport, the little village of **Litton Cheney** nestles at the foot of the hills. The area is rich is prehistoric remains with numerous barrows, tumuli, earthworks and standing stones. Easily reached along a pleasant coast walk from Bridport or West Bay is **Burton Bradstock**, a delightfully unspoiled example of a rural Dorset village and a great attraction for artists and visitors from the nearby resorts. Here picturesque thatched cottages and inns line the narrow, twisting lanes, one of which leads down to a little sandy beach backed by cliffs. Burton Bradstock church is also of interest, containing communion rails dated 1686 and some unusual painted panelling.

◁ Litton Cheney
Old cottages, Burton Bradstock ▷

The harbour-road soon began to justify its name. A gap appeared in the rampart of hills which shut out the sea, and on the left of the opening rose a vertical cliff, coloured a burning orange by the sunlight, the companion cliff on the right being livid in shade

Fellow-Townsmen

The ancient town of **Bridport**, the "Port Bredy" of Hardy's novels, was famous for its rope-making industry, to which it owes the width of its thoroughfares which were used as rope-walks. The 18th century Town Hall which overlooks the cross-roads in the centre of the town is a pleasing building of Georgian design. Some two miles south of Bridport is the popular little resort of **West Bay.** It faces the great sweep of Lyme Bay and the harbour, at the mouth of the River Brit, was built in 1740 to serve inland Bridport. In the 19th century it was a busy ship-building port where schooners and naval vessels continued to be built until 1879; now it provides a haven for small boats. The cliffs in the environs of West Bay are worn into a series of ledges by the effect of erosion on the alternating bands of hard and soft rock.

◁ Town Hall, Bridport
A stormy day, West Bay ▷

The elegant and dignified town of Lyme Regis looks out across the wide expanse of **Lyme Bay** which has been the location for many historic events including the landfall of the Duke of Monmouth in 1685 at the start of his unsuccessful rebellion. The bay is backed by crumbling sandstone cliffs which are a famous hunting ground for fossil collectors and provide breathtaking views along the coast. The cliffs culminate in the glowing sandstone peak of **Golden Cap**, the highest point on England's southern coast. It reaches a height of some 620 feet and is now part of a vast estate protected by the National Trust.

◁ Lyme Bay from Golden Cap

Golden Cap ▷

Set below steep hills, **Lyme Regis** is an elegant old town with twisting, narrow streets, dignified Georgian houses and an attractive promenade. The town can date its origin to AD 774 when the King of the West Saxons granted local monks the right to extract salt from sea water. It was under Edward I, who used Lyme as a base for his wars against France, that 'Regis' was added to its name. During the 18th century the town became a fashionable seaside resort and was a favourite place of Jane Austen who set part of her novel *Persuasion* in the town. No longer a commercial port, the attractive harbour is still well used by fishing boats and private craft. It is protected by the 14th century stone breakwater which is known as the Cobb.

◁ The Cobb, Lyme Regis
Lyme Regis harbour ▷

" *At this moment of the morning Angel Clare was riding along a narrow lane in the direction of his father's vicarage at Emminster. ...His father's hill-surrounded little town, the Tudor church-tower of red stone, the clump of trees near the vicarage, came at last into view beneath him, and he rode down towards the well-known gate.* "

Tess of the d'Urbervilles

Built in terraces on the side of the hill, **Powerstock** is overshadowed by 827 feet high Eggardon Hill which is crowned by an Iron Age fort. Stone cottages, some of them thatched, and fine houses are grouped around the Church of St. Mary, a Norman structure which was extensively rebuilt in Victorian times. It retains some fine 15th century carvings and in the churchyard stands the stone table which was used as early as the 13th century for the distribution of bread to the poor. Delightfully situated in a natural amphitheatre sheltered by surrounding hills **Beaminster**, which featured as Emminster in Hardy's *Tess of the d'Urbervilles*, lies in an area of outstanding natural beauty. Streets radiate from the attractive Square which is lined by handsome 18th century houses and the little River Brit runs alongside the main street. The church is held to be one of the best in Dorset and the highly ornamented tower, built of golden Ham Hill stone, dates from Tudor times.

◁ Powerstock
Beaminster ▷

> *Three miles further she cut across the straight and deserted Roman road called Long-Ash Lane; leaving which as soon as she reached it she dipped down a hill by a transverse lane into the small town or village of Evershead... She made a halt here, and breakfasted a second time, heartily enough — not at the Sow-and-Acorn, for she avoided inns, but at a cottage by the church.*

Tess of the d'Urbervilles

The village of **Godmanstone** lies in the attractive Cerne Valley not far from Dorchester. Here stands the Smith's Arms, a 17th century building of flint and stone which is reputed to be the smallest inn in England. It consists of a single room which measures 39 feet long by 14 feet wide and is only 12 feet high. According to legend it was first licenced by King Charles II who stopped at the smithy to have his horse shod and granted a licence so that he could also have a drink. South of Yeovil there are a number of delightful little villages nestling among wooded hills and approached along winding lanes where wild flowers grow in profusion in spring and summer. Traditionally, cottages such as these at **Evershot** are thatched with Dorset reed which gives a smoother finish than ordinary straw thatch. Evershot is the "Evershead" of Tess of the d'Urbervilles.

◁ The Smith's Arms, Godmanstone
Cottage at Evershot ▷

Best known for its white hillside figure of the Cerne Giant, the village of **Cerne Abbas**, "Abbot's Cernal" in Far from the Madding Crowd, is itself exceptionally beautiful. Among its many interesting old buildings is the gatehouse of the 10th century abbey, at one time one of the most important in the south of England. There is also an attractive row of half-timbered cottages standing near the church in Abbey Street. Situated in a peaceful valley enclosed by wooded slopes, the unspoilt village of **Milton Abbas**, Hardy's "Middleton Abbey" from The Woodlanders, has a long curving street lined by ancient thatched cottages. It was created as an 18th century model village when the first Earl of Dorchester, to protect his privacy, demolished the old houses which surrounded Milton Abbey and built a new village on a site nearby. The Benedictine abbey church dates from the 14th century.

◁ Cerne Abbas

Milton Abbas ▷

A town of considerable historical and architectural interest **Sherborne**, the "Sherton Abbas" of Thomas Hardy, is set amongst green hills on the River Yeo. There are many notable old buildings in the town including the splendid Abbey Church. The present structure, which dates mainly from the 15th century, replaced an earlier one and retains a fine Saxon doorway as well as a tenor bell given to the abbey by Cardinal Wolsey. The Choir is said to be the finest example of Perpendicular work in existence. Fine old houses and shops built, like the abbey, in golden Ham Hill stone line the main street and at the foot of Cheap Street is a 14th century conduit which was once a wash-house and stood within the cloisters of the Abbey Church.

" *Thus talking they reached the ancient town of Sherton Abbas. By no pressure would she ride up the street with him....He blushed a little, shook his head at her, and drove on ahead into the streets; the churches, the abbey, and other medieval buildings on this clear bright morning having the linear distinctness of architectural drawings, as if the original dream and vision of the conceiving master-mason were for a brief hour flashed down through the centuries to an unappreciative age.* "

The Woodlanders

◁ The Conduit, Sherborne
The Parade, Sherborne ▷

The village of Marlott lay amid the north-eastern undulations of the beautiful Vale of Blakemore or Blackmoor. ...This fertile and sheltered tract of country, in which the fields are never brown and the springs never dry, is bounded on the south by the bold chalk ridge that embraces the prominences of Hambledon Hill, Bulbarrow, Nettlecombe-Tout, Dogbury, High Stoy, and Bubb Down. The atmosphere beneath is languorous, and is so tinged with azure that what artists call the middle distance partakes also of that hue, while the horizon beyond is of the deepest ultramarine. Arable lands are few and limited; with but slight exceptions the prospect is a broad mass of grass and trees, mantling minor hills and dales within the major. Such is the Vale of Blackmoor. "

Tess of the d'Urbervilles.

The ancient town of **Shaftesbury**, "Shaston" in Tess of the d'Ubervilles, crowns a high spur of land overlooking Blackmore Vale to the south. Its commanding position led Alfred the Great to choose the site as one of the principal towns in his kingdom of Wessex. It was he who founded Shaftesbury Abbey, the ruins of which still survive. Today Shaftesbury is rich in historical remains and its most famous and picturesque landmark is Gold Hill. This ancient cobbled street leads steeply down from the present day High Street and affords magnificent views over Blackmore Vale. First records of Gold Hill date from 1362 when most of the street was called Long Hill, only the topmost part near the Town Hall being known as Gold Hill. With its pretty tiled and thatched cottages on one side and massive medieval buttressed wall on the other, Gold Hill is a fascinating reminder of Shaftesbury's historic past.

◁ Gold Hill, Shaftesbury
Blackmore Vale ▷

An important market town from early times, **Blandford Forum** was largely destroyed by fire in 1731 and the re-built town is an outstanding example of classical Georgian architecture. The imposing buildings which surround the market place owe their handsome appearance to the work of two brothers who were local builders. Blandford features in the novels of Thomas Hardy as "Shottsford Forum". **Okeford Fitzpaine** lies between Blandford and Sturminster Newton. Described in The Woodlanders as "Oakbury Fitzpiers", the village is an excellent centre for walks with footpaths and bridle ways traversing the north-facing escarpment of the Dorset hills. Nearby Okeford Hill rises to 739 feet and provides panoramic views of the downs.

◁ Blandford Forum
Okeford Fitzpaine ▷

> *Standing on the top of a giant's grave in*
> *this antique land, Ethelberta lifted her eyes*
> *to behold two sorts of weather pervading*
> *nature at the same time. Far below on the*
> *right hand it was a fine day, and the silver*
> *sunbeams lighted up a many-armed inland*
> *sea, which stretched round an island*
> *with fir trees and gorse, and amid brilliant*
> *crimson heaths wherein white paths and roads*
> *occasionally met the eye in dashes and*
> *zigzags like flashes of lightning*

The Hand of Ethelberta.

The broad arc of Poole Bay stretches from Hengistbury Head in the east to Poole Harbour in the west, lined by some of the most popular beaches in the south of England. **Poole**, Hardy's "Havenpool", situated on one of the largest shallow-water anchorages in Britain, has always been an important port and it is a superb location for the yachtsmen who throng there in the summer. One of the largest towns in the county, Poole is a much-loved resort with fine parks and sandy beaches. The heart of the town centres around the harbour where numerous buildings of historic interest stand on the busy quayside. These include 15th century warehouses, a fine 18th century Guildhall, which now houses a museum of local history, and the splendid Custom House with its distinctive double flight of steps.

◁ Sunset, Poole Harbour
Church Street, Poole ▷

" *This fashionable watering-place, with its*
eastern and its western stations, its piers, its
groves of pines, its promenades, and its covered
gardens, was, to Angel Clare, like a fairy place
suddenly created by the stroke of a wand, and
allowed to get a little dusty. It was a city of
detatched mansions; a Mediterranean lounging-
place on the English Channel; and as seen now
by night it seemed even more imposing than
it was. The sea was near at hand, but not
intrusive: it murmured, and he thought it was
the pines; the pines murmured in precisely the
same tones, and he thought they were the sea. "

Tess of the d'Urbervilles.

Ideally situated on a magnificent bay facing the Channel, **Bournemouth** is one of the country's leading resorts. Together with its neighbouring town of Boscombe it offers sandy beaches, cliffs and wooded chines as well as two piers and a wide range of seaside amusements. The beach, sheltered by 100 feet high cliffs, is reached by means of the East Cliff Lift or by shady paths which wind through chines cut into the cliffs. Bournemouth also has a well-used International Centre and numerous delightful gardens and open spaces. Along with the Lower and Upper Gardens, the colourful Central Gardens extend along the little Bourne Valley to the seafront where the Pavilion Rock Gardens also provide refuge for those who want an alternative to the beach.

◁ Sunrise, Bournemouth
Late afternoon, Poole Bay ▷

Copying architecture in an Old Minster (Wimborne)

How smartly the quarters of the hour march by
That the jack-o'-clock never forgets;
Ding-dong; and before I have traced a cusp's eye,
Or got the true twist of the ogee over,
A double ding-dong ricochetts.

Just so did he clang here before I came,
And so will he clang when I'm gone
Through the Minster's cavernous hollows — the same
Tale of hours never more to be will he deliver
To the speechless midnight and dawn!

Complete Poems

Wimborne Minster, the "Warborne" of Two on a Tower, was originally founded as a nunnery in 713 AD and the beautiful Minster Church of St. Cuthburga dominates this peaceful market town. Rebuilt in the 12th century, the Minster embraces many architectural styles and among its items of historic interest are an astronomical clock believed to date from 1325, a notable chained library and a Quarter Jack in the form of a grenadier which strikes the bell on the west tower marking the quarter hours. Just outside the town, the ancient village of **Pamphill** lies in a valley between the Rivers Stour and Allen. Here is a charming group of sturdy cottages with thick walls and neatly thatched roofs adjoin the picturesque green.

◁ Julian's Bridge, Wimborne Minster
The Green, Pamphill ▷